DEDICATION

This book is dedicated to entrepreneurs whose perseverance and fortitude continue to be the forefront of business ownership. Write the vision and make it plain. You will reach your achievements and become a success in any business you desire.

Acknowledgments

Appreciations are extended to Audra Marshall and Under His Wings Executive Services, for working with me to ensure that this book was completed. I am thankful to my husband for serving as my mentor.

Throughout this process, my husband, Kevin Davis was available for direction, support, and words of reassurance. It has been an honor and privilege to work with him all during this journey. Finally, I want to thank the Photographers whose pictures I was able to use from the website Pexels. You kept the cost low and allowed me to move forward with my book.

CONTENTS

BEING A VISIONARY AND GOING AFTER YOUR VISION

Who Is A Visionary?

A Visionary is a person who has lots of ideas, is a strategic thinker, always sees the big picture, has a pulse on your industry, connects the dots, and researches and develops new products and services.

The Visionary typically is the founding entrepreneur, operates more on emotion, and has ADD (but not always). This person is great with big relationships, the culture of the organization, and solving big, ugly problems (not the little ones), sees things others can't, creates and holds the company vision, and is great at closing big deals. Visionaries are paramount for the success of any society.

The idea here is that if you are a Visionary, your job is to delegate and elevate yourself to your true God-given skill set. This will require you to have a strong Integrator in place so that you can fully assume the Visionary role for your organization. This will free up your energy and creativity to grow your company, protect your vision, your customers, get more business, protect your culture, and stay three steps ahead of everyone, including the competition. A visionary creates himself first, and formats his mind to work through time, capturing all the ideas, concepts, and innovations from all areas, anywhere he can. We then build upon these and add to them. Then we project them into a future perfect setting. We are relentless in our pursuit, and tireless in our passion.

A visionary is a creative genius who refuses to accept things as they are. They are the proverbial "Unreasonable Man." They look at the world and say, "this isn't good enough" and commit themselves to making it better. They never stop asking why things are the way they are and "What If" we did this instead.

One caution: It's vital that, as a Visionary, you work closely with and trust your Integrator because your Integrator will serve as a great filter of all your ideas and protect the company from the chaos. Its vital because your company can only move as fast as its capacity.

Side Note on the Perfect Integrator

My husband and I started our business in 2008. At that time, I worked full time and managed our business part-time. I was able to do this because I had an integrator (Door Keeper) who was awesome at her job. Audra answered the phone, set the appointments, and confirmed the appointments. We both worked with our clients and our clients did not know that we were not a full time business. I went on appointments after work and met clients in Starbucks or my friend's real estate office. This went on for several years until my company made enough money to acquire office space. Audra still works from home but the time and dedication she devotes to our business is invaluable; I could not put a price tag on it. If you plan to spend money on any position in your company, you need to spend the money on this kind of key personnel. When we started in 2008, I could not pay my Integrator, Audra, her worth but she hung in there with us and now she is still that integral person who holds our business together. I feel her worth is still more than what we can ever pay her, but her dedication to our company is mainly why we are so successful today.

What Does It Mean To Be A Visionary Business Leader?

Vision in business requires that you clearly see where you choose to be in future and formulate the necessary steps to get your organization there. Creating and sustaining a vision for an organization calls for discipline and creativity. A business

leader must have the passion, strength of will, and necessary knowledge to achieve long-term goals. A focused individual who can inspire his team to reach organizational goals is a visionary business leader.

How Can A Business Leader Turn Vision Into Reality?

Whenever a vision is followed by action, the vision can be turned into reality. One important action of leadership is the formation of a formidable team. No single skill set is sufficient in achieving success in business. A visionary leader recognizes talent and recruits individuals with skills that complement each other and contribute to business growth.

Before any action can be turned into reality, a great deal of discipline is necessary. Discipline requires that you follow through with your purpose and direction, even in the face of obstacles and setbacks. This may require the leader to take responsibility for the team's actions and decisions.

A visionary leader turns vision into reality by creating a vivid image of the target they need to attain and creating a specific strategic plan for the coming year. The leader details what goals the company must accomplish and the specific responsibilities of each key team member. Along the way, the leader keeps the team informed of their progress and the leader celebrates small victories with the team, while remaining focused on the big goal.

Going After Your Vision:
Steps To Be Taken To Go After Your Vision

- ## Ignore the reality of present circumstances

What's happening today does not dictate your future.

No matter how bad things are now, you'll acknowledge it and ignore it. The present circumstances are temporary and fleeting. Imagine you're in an elevator and want to get to the top floor; your present circumstances are on the first floor.

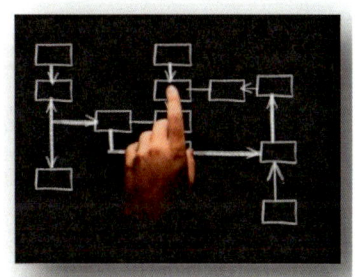

The fact that you're on the first floor doesn't mean your elevator isn't about to shoot up. Your life is about to change very quickly but you must not let the present circumstances trick you into believing your life is in a dismal condition.

- ## Get clear on what you want

You won't know what floor you want the elevator to take you to until you press the floor you want. Similarly, you won't know how to get there if you don't know where you want to go in the first place.

Without direction and guidance, it will take you where it wants to take you but life always waits for your direction. You must dream it and see it in your mind and visualize it. Let life know what you want; let life know what you want your future to look like.

• Imagine you are already there

Regardless of the present circumstances, change your life to start reflecting your future reality. You may not have the love of your life, be living in your dream city or doing the work you love, but you can cultivate those feelings you desire.

Do you desire love, freedom, adventure, companionship, friendship, personal growth and more? You can achieve those feelings today! Go out with a friend you haven't met up with in some time. Take a day trip to a famous spot around town. Sightsee in your own city. Take a staycation. Visit beauty and nature where you are.

• Cultivate joyful vibrations

Every day you can choose how you feel and how you view the world. You can actively change the way you feel by focusing on the good things. You can change the way you feel by experiencing gratitude. You can change the way you feel by listening to inspiring music, reading positive books and listening to inspiring podcasts. You can also take proactive actions to kill the negativity in your life.

Stop doing stuff that tears your soul and reduce the time you spend with intolerable people. Seek a different workplace if you're not in good energy at work. As far as viewing the world, you must believe you have the power of perception. You can't change the circumstances of your life but you can change your view of those circumstances. You can see your life through the lens of negativity or you can see your life through the lens of growth, inspiration, adventure, change, and transformation. However you see your life, your life will respond accordingly.

- **Take steps to get to the place you envision**

From knowing your vision and cultivating positive vibrations, and from a place of possibility, take steps every day towards your dreams. Create habits so you have a systematic way to move towards your dream life every day. If you're an artist, create art every day. If you're an entrepreneur, work on your business every day. If you're a writer, write every day. If you're an athlete, work out every day. Your dream life doesn't happen if you simply envision it; it requires inspired action.

Work backwards from your dream life to the one thing you can do today to move towards that life. What one small step can you take each and every day that will move you closer to the life you want? You can create your future life one day at a time, starting today.

- **Surrender**

Work on the parts of your dreams you can, but surrender on the results; don't fixate on the results themselves or on your dream life. This will happen naturally if you focus on the journey. Work on creating  your dream life every day and before you know it you'll materialize it. Know where you want to go, work on getting there, take inspired action every day but surrender to the universe on the time and place. Life will get you there in due time. If you do your part, life will do its part. You don't have to control, force or manipulate the universe. You don't have to fear, worry or doubt. If you trust the journey, your destination will appear soon enough.

- **Believe every event is moving you closer to your vision**

Every setback, every challenge and every obstacle is preparing you for your dream. Life is simply testing you to see if you believe strongly enough in your vision. Most people give up quickly and think they must live the difficult life they've received.

Challenges and obstacles are tests. Your ability to overcome the challenges in your path will give you the skills to achieve your dreams. You only have to learn and grow from the obstacles in front of you, while not taking your eyes away from the prize.

Most people let obstacles discourage them and believe life wants them to choose different direction. Don't mistake a test that will strengthen you for a challenge that will doom you. Your vision for your life is divinely inspired and universally supported. You must bring your resilience, persistence and faith.

Side Note On Business Failure

Business failure sets one up for success. Sometimes it is not failure that is happening, but at the time it feels like it is. When we first started our business in 2008, we joined a multilevel marketing company and I helped my clients with their personal financial goals by setting them up with a systematic way to achieve their goals. It always started with securing the framework by obtaining life insurance and then we dealt with their credit and then saving money for their future. It was a good foundation but what I found was as soon as something upset the apple cart, as I use to say, everything crashed down and the first thing to go was the insurance, then the savings. Sure, I made money on selling the product but it broke my heart to see that their future was at risk.

 Additionally, I found that this multi-level marketing format was not for me as I was not the hard seller that I needed to be. Therefore, our organization switched gears and started working with businesses and helping organizations to become profitable. I enjoy this much more and there really is not any hard selling as the company has one choice; to follow the plan if they want to stay in business.

Therefore, switching from personal financial clients to business clients was not a failure, although at the time, it felt like it. I learned so much from the multi-level marketing company; some things I use today in my business and those things have helped my company grow into the six-million-dollar company it is today.

Missions and Visions will change early in a business venture, so allow yourself to do that and not look at it as a complete failure, but as a learning experience that can move your business to the next level.

How To Succeed As A Visionary

One very important success factor in life is your ability to carry a noble vision in your heart. A visionary is a man or woman with a vision to excel in an aspect of life or living. Most people who

succeed as founders of some great companies or organizations are most times visionary leaders.

Their finding success is not by accident; they took time and put in effort to develop their abilities to create useful changes in our world.

Although visionaries are dreamers, they are more than idle dreamers because they move to become leaders in their chosen line of business or careers; by doing what it takes to make their dreams a reality. Getting to know how they succeeded as listed below could be the pathway to success of anyone aspiring to become a successful visionary too.

As leaders, visionaries acquire useful information relevant to their chosen field; this helps them stay ahead of the crowd. Succeeding as a visionary requires that you know more and do more than

others in order to be ahead of them. The patronage you receive and the following you command in your chosen line of expertise sometimes is a clue that people need your products or services; your continuity and improvement upon it could be rewarded.

Successful visionary leaders most times have their eyes and ears to the ground; this means that they are very observant and are quick to identify current trends in their areas of interest. And with the facts gained, they are able to predict the most likely profitable direction to head for.

Succeeding in business as a visionary requires resourcefulness and this ability to find solutions quickly, to challenges encountered on the way, is acquired by engaging in sound analytical and logical thinking. This is one of the key success habits of visionary leaders; the habit of leaving no stone unturned whenever they need a solution to any challenge.

The path of success as a visionary leader in any aspect of life is not devoid of mental and physical diligence. Mental diligence means having the ability to meditate on your ideas, brainstorm and follow through on them. Succeeding as a visionary leader in your chosen field means you are aware that your job or aim is to turn abstract intangibles in the mental or spiritual realm into tangible and physical best selling products or services.

You must, therefore, be a tireless researcher so that you can always come forth with fresh ideas for innovative products and ideas. You must also possess the dogged determination to pursue your dream, alone, in the early stages of launching until you have adequately displayed enough proof that you're indeed an authority in that field.

Above all these listed above, an intense belief and trust in the Most High God is of paramount importance to succeeding as visionary; knowing that you're not a success because you are the most intelligent or smartest worker in that field. You attain success by God's grace alone. Due to the magnitude of work that an aspiring visionary leader has to put in especially in the early stages of their venture; most people shy away from pursuing their noble dreams. Ironically, the world today is in dire need of such successful visionaries in almost any field you could think of. They set the pace for great changes. You could be the next great visionary the world is waiting for if only you would apply yourself and dare to make that dream in your heart for a better world come true.

Benefits Of A Visionary

In this fast-paced technological age that increasingly demands change, being a visionary is a must for survival and success. It is often observed that many companies come into play and become successful and profitable for a short while, but then they fall badly when they face the first storm. A big percentage of such companies do not even survive. They disappear. Why? The main reason is that they do not have visionary leaders. Being a visionary in whatever you do whether as a CEO, a manager, a team leader, a supervisor, a business owner, an employee,a professional worker, a doctor, a dentist, an engineer, a lawyer, a community volunteer, a coach, a teacher, a husband, or a wife is very beneficial for you and others.

Here Are Some Benefits Of Being A Visionary

- **You see the big picture**

Visionary people are big picture people, they do not get stuck with unnecessary details. Unlike ordinary leaders, visionary leaders can easily zoom out and see the big picture. They are like a proficient painter who, once in a while, zooms out and looks at his creation from a distance to see how perfect it is and how close his creation is to the picture in his mind.

As a visionary leader, by looking at the big picture you become detached from what is going on. As a result you will be able to link various events with one another and take proactive actions before problems show up. You are always ahead of the game because, in the big picture, you can also see your final destination.

As a leader who sees the big picture, you take ultimate responsibility for what happens along the way.

- **Your ultimate goal is clear to yourself and others**

Visionary leaders have a definite and clear vision. When the vision is clear, the ultimate goal is also clear not only to you but also to those whom you lead. Having a clear and powerful ultimate goal is crucial in motivating people to strive for achieving that goal. This is a great benefit that by being a visionary you can possess.

Side Note On Goals

How many of you have heard of SMART Goal Setting?

SMART stands for:
- Specific
- Motivational
- Action-oriented
- Relevant to your situation
- Time-bound

and is a useful acronym for making sure you're setting goals that are actually achievable.

Business goals follow the same goal setting rules as personal goals.

They, too, need to be relevant, actionable and "achievable stretches." Business goals, of course, are an inherent part of business planning.

I conduct a Workshop titled "The Business Makeover." I help entrepreneurs create a Business Action Plan that will provide business direction for a year or longer.

These are small workshops no more then 6-8 entrepreneurs at a time so that when completed, you will have a Vision Statement, a Mission Statement and specific business goals that enable you to put your business planning into action. Having business goals are important but having SMART business goals set your business up for success.

- **You become more focused**

What matters is the ability to focus on the worthy. When you focus your energy on what matters, you do not become distracted by external forces. As a result, you always have your vision and your ultimate goal in mind and you remain focused as well, no matter how difficult the situation is.

- **You are not disappointed with temporary setbacks**

Since visionary leaders constantly have their vision in mind and focus on the ultimate goal for their organization, they do not become disappointed with temporary setbacks.

Visionary leaders never give up; they learn valuable lessons from failures and never make a mistake twice. Everyone may fall, but falling forward is a benefit. As a visionary leader, you may fall but you must stand up right away and move forward because you have a clear vision in front of you. The attitude of not becoming disappointed with temporary setbacks gives the visionary leader the courage to take risks, transform those risks to opportunities, and eventually earn the rewards.

- **You become a searchlight for others to follow**

 Visionary leaders are the ones who take the road less travelled. They are even the ones who may discover the paths untraveled. Once they discover an untraveled path, they become searchlights by highlighting the path for others to follow. As a visionary leader, you say no to following the crowd and as a result you become worthy of being followed by the crowd.

Qualities Of How To Be A Good Visionary

Everyone has a purpose and everyone has been given vision, however; great vision is usually given to those who have the wider scope and having the wider scope is a choice. Having a great vision has nothing to do with who is better than who, or who has the most talent; instead all of those who have been given great vision have at least one thing in common and that is their vision is fuelled in the thoughts of bringing solutions to others.

These great visionaries have the hugest hearts and wear their hearts out in the open. In fact every great visionary that we have learned about happens to be a huge giver; they're not afraid to be vulnerable and they will often times put their trust in people who would never do the same. History shares with us how many great visionaries were often betrayed by their closest allies, but there is one thing we noticed, it is that they  never stop giving. Why? Just why were these great visionaries willing to put their name, or their life, on the line with no guarantees?

It might seem difficult to understand, but if studied you will notice the same thing runs through each and every one of them. Their focus is always on the fact that they are the vessel. It is with the ability to surrender their selfish desires to aid a greater purpose that they are lifted to heights that give them a greater awareness and a view that is literally irreversible.

Having had their vision expanded to see the possibilities that would occur through them if they were only willing, compels them to achieve feats that most of us will only read about long after it has happened or in our history books. Many of us will have even rubbed shoulders with budding great visionaries, but because our vision is limited we miss them and ultimately miss the message they bring.

However, make no mistake, everyone is capable of being a great visionary, but many will never look beyond their own reach to see it. So why are they given great visions? These visionaries can be trusted because of their willingness; having been tested, they are humble enough to learn from others and so are given the ability to lead others. They don't seek greatness just to say they are great, they seek greatness because they have been given a vision of greatness and have a great desire to lift others to greatness. They want for others what they want for themselves and they spend their lives creating ways to do that.

To all of us who are budding great visionaries let us remember, the size of our vision has always been and will always be up to us. What we create is up to us. What we allow to flow through us is up to us. Our willingness is like a huge vessel connected to us; and those that allow that vessel to be expanded are given the greatest visions.

Steps To Be Taken To Become A Visionary Person

- **Appreciate people**

This means ALL people, not just certain people you care about. Each and every person on Earth has a special mission or a unique purpose in life. Learn to appreciate the special and not so special talents, skills, and personalities of others because you never know what lesson you'll learn from them.

- **Accept responsibility**

You should never accept the position that you're a victim of circumstance. You alone are responsible for the things you experience, the choices you make, and the outcomes of those choices and experiences. Placing blame on others for your choices or mistakes is not only childish, but will prevent you from learning from these mistakes and improving your life.

- **Strive to learn and improve**

You should know and understand that the job of self-improvement is never ending. It's a constant cycle, and it revolves consistently as we advance through life. Working to improve yourself, the lives of those around you and the world will make you one of the top visionaries that the world has ever seen. By taking steps to improve yourself and looking for ways to improve the world, you'll begin to think about solutions more creatively.

- **Discover the positive effect of challenges**

You must understand and approach all situations as if they're a lesson and you should always strive to learn something from them. Transform your thinking from believing that something is bad to believing that no matter how negative it appears at first glance; there is ultimately something positive to be gained from it.

- **Take action to make your dreams come true**

Last, but not least, if you're seeking to become a visionary, you must be both a dreamer and a doer. It's wonderful to set goals and have dreams, but if you never put anything into action, the thoughts and dreams are futile.

Side Note On Always Improving Yourself

At the time of this writing, I have completed my Bachelors, Masters, and a Doctoral Program, in which this educational journey started at the age of 40. Yes, I started my educational journey right out of high school, but at that time I was not focused on education; my life took many twists and turns to where I am today.

Completing my bachelors at 40, and in two years, started because the Human Resources Manager of an organization that hired me questioned why I did not have my degree. I thought about it and started back to school just to complete my bachelor's degree. At the time, I interviewed for the position I asked for a salary of six figures and even though I did not get it, but got close to it, I felt that they would have given it to me if I had my degree. So, I went back to school, attending Thomas Edison College, which is now Thomas Edison University. This school was an online, distant learning school and doing it this way allowed me to still work, and be a wife, mother, manage the business and carry on with my other responsibilities. I finished in two years. Along the way, a good friend came on the journey and we graduated together. She then needed her Master's degree in pursuit of her career goals, I joined her in attending Walden University, and we received our Master's degrees in two years as well. It was her bright idea to get our Doctorate degrees and I went along hesitantly. However, after graduating from Walden University, I am glad I did as this journey has taught me so much about business and life. The education is irreplaceable to me now. Improving myself this way has opened doors for me in business and networking relationships. These doors would not have opened if I did not have the degrees that I have accomplished. I am still improving myself by staying current and joining organizations to stay up-to-date on business issues. I feel that it is one's responsibility to oneself, one's clients, one's team, and the organization that one has built or is building to always improve oneself and ones worth.

Important Characteristics Of Business Visionaries

When passion is combined with an effective strategy, it can generate an unstoppable force. Business visionaries are more than just dreamers, they are practical people who solve problems, recognize obstacles, and know how to deal with failure. Anyone can dream big, but it is only the visionary who is capable of turning big ideas into reality. We are lucky enough to have many of the most successful business visionaries of all time alive today. These inspirational people are the perfect role models to learn from because they have a proven track-record of success. It's probably not going to be possible to become a carbon copy of one of these visionaries, but it is possible to develop the characteristics that led them to greatness.

The people who are able to turn dreams into something physical vary greatly in personality and temperament. All of them have their own unique personality quirks, and they'd also probably admit to having some bad habits. There are certain characteristics that these visionaries tend to share and here are just eight of them.

Here Are Some Characteristics Of A Business Visionary

- **Drive to succeed**

Ideas without the passion to make them happen

are like cars without gas – they don't go anywhere. Business visionaries succeed because they have the passion to put in the necessary effort needed to create something real. The thing that made it possible for someone like Sergey Brin to

create something new and exciting in the world was his ability to come up with interesting ideas. If he hadn't helped to create Google, it's almost certain that something similar would have been created by somebody else.

- **Clear vision**

Entrepreneurs who don't have a clear vision can easily be knocked off track. This can mean an approach to business that is unfocused, erratic, and sloppy. If you don't know where you want to go, how do you hope to get there? It is not possible to be a business visionary without a clear vision for the future. Your goal needs to be more precise than the vague hope of building a successful business. You need to have targets that are measurable, achievable, and easy to explain to other people.

- **Determination to do whatever it takes**

There is no big secret as to why business visionaries are able to achieve so much – their success is earned by doing what other people are not prepared to do. Maybe a few entrepreneurs can make an impact from the comfort of a hammock on a tropical island, active only for a four-hour work week, but this is the rare exception and not the rule. If you are serious about leaving your mark on the world, you need to be willing to work much harder than the average person. You also need to understand that being 'good' is probably not going to be enough to get you where you want to go; your aim should be to become the best.

- ## Ability to inspire other people

If you can't get the rest of your team to see the value in your vision, they are not going to be able to fully commit to the project. This is why it is so important to have a clear goal, and you also need to be able to communicate to other people why it is going to be worthwhile. It is also going to help if you openly express your passion and enthusiasm because these characteristics can be highly contagious. It is worth spending some time writing down your thoughts about how your vision is going to change the world and help other people. If your vision is only about making you feel good, it's unlikely to inspire your team.

- ## Resilience in the face of failure

All true business visionaries are going to need to deal with significant failure in their career, usually more than once. It is only when people experience things going wrong that they truly get to see if they have the right characteristics to be a business visionary.  Resilience in the face of failure means that these entrepreneurs use this experience as a chance to learn and grow. They can do this because of their insight that mistakes and wrong turns are just part of the journey.

- **Willingness to be a team player**

The benefit of working as part of a team is that it means there is going to be the right people to make up for the skills you lack. If you try to do everything yourself, the results are likely to be amateurish. The characteristics of an effective team player would include the ability to listen, the willingness to compromise, and the openness to have your ideas challenged.

- **Side Note On Having The Perfect Team**

Having the perfect team in business is key to business growth. When we were starting out and even now, each person on our organization team knows what his or her assignment is and does it well. Even down to my husband who signs the checks every month and accompanies me on my speaking engagements; his assignment is just as important as Audra's who sets up the engagements, makes sure I have everything I need, and does pre and post follow up. Her position has grown so much that we are looking to hire her an assistant so that she can stay in the position that she is in. The old adage, "Teamwork Makes the Dream Work" is so true. Moreover, this type of philosophy allows me to be the visionary of the organization, which produces growth in our organization.

- ## Mentally Flexible Enough To Change Course

Effective business visionaries are focused on a clear goal, but they are not inflexible when it comes to the path to this goal. It is easy to take a wrong turn in business, but this doesn't have to be disastrous, as long as you are always willing to change course and admit mistakes. Even if your strategy is the right one, you are still probably going to need to make a few adjustments to it in order to get to where you want to go. Many businesses have failed because managers refused to recognize that they had gone off-track.

- ## Courage To Act From Intuition

Don't let the noise of others' opinions drown out your own inner voice. Most importantly, have the courage to follow your heart and intuition. Sometimes you may be faced with a situation where all your advisors are telling you one thing, but your gut is telling you something else. Even if you can't clearly explain why your solution is the right one, you ignore your intuition at your peril.

This inner-voice benefits from all of your knowledge and experience in life up until now – it is the most trustworthy advisor you are ever going to find. Just be careful that you don't mistake your ego for your intuition.

Side Note On Courage To Act From Intuition

Intuition? I call it being led by a high calling. When I have speaking engagements I always tell my audience to know what time of day they  get understanding about their business. For me, it is early morning and I keep pen and paper near my bed to write down the things that I believe the calling is telling me to do. It could be a specific task for the day or an overall reaching direction for the organization as a whole.

The point is, when I know I get this direction NO ONE can veer me from going in that direction. Usually, the key players in the organization align with the direction and that gives me confirmation that we are to do it. However, with or without their confirmation, I move forward.

 Some call it intuition and for this book, that I hope reaches the masses in business development, you can call it whatever you want. For me, I call it the higher calling that has guided this business into the business it is today and I would not have it any other way. It is my most trustworthy advisor and the best part of this is that it is free advice because I have chosen this path for my life.

There are many ways to get in touch with us, so please do not hesitate to email, phone, visit our website or mail

We are here to help!

Contact Us:

 millicentdavis@kmdbusinessconsultants.com

 856-318-9034

 www.millicentdavis.com

 2030 N. Black Horse Pike Williamstown, NJ

 @TakingControlOfYourDestiny

For general information, or to share your testimony, and or if you would like Dr. Davis to speak at your function email Dr. Davis at: millicentdavis@kmdbusinessconsultants.com

Made in United States
North Haven, CT
23 November 2021

11431296R00020